I0821930

YOUCAT

Confession

ihs
יהוה

YOUCAT

ENGLISH

CONFESSION

Archbishop Salvatore Cordileone
Auxiliary Bishop Emeritus Dr. Klaus Dick
Rudolf Gehrig
Bernhard Meuser
Fr. Andreas Süss

IGNATIUS PRESS SAN FRANCISCO

Nihil Obstat: Adrian Walker, Ph.D.

Imprimatur: † Most Rev. Salvatore J. Cordileone,
Archbishop of San Francisco, December 19, 2024

Original German edition, *YOUCAT Update! Beichten!*,

www.youcat.org

Design, layout, illustrations: Alexander von Lengerke, Cologne, Germany

Published in 2025 by Ignatius Press, San Francisco

Printed in Canada

ISBN 978-1-62164-294-7

ISBN 978-1-64229-141-4 (eBook)

Library of Congress Control Number 2019932006

Symbols and their meaning:

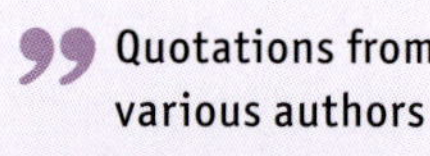

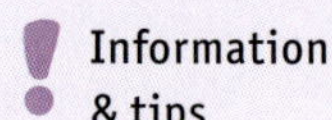

Contents

INSTEAD OF A FOREWORD

When I was fifteen years old, I had experienced very little of the truly liberating effect of confession. But a lot has happened since then. I became a priest and now enjoy being able to show young people the beauty of God's love and mercy in the sacrament of reconciliation—and to experience this myself time and again in my own confessions. I have been privileged to hear countless confessions from young people, and it moves me deeply to see how God frees us from guilt, heals wounds, and enables us to experience new life through his forgiveness.

Before World Youth Day in 2005, I would never have imagined that young people could be happy to spend six hours together praying and singing and then going to confession. Yet this is precisely what happened to a group of young people from Bonn who attended World Youth Day in Cologne, and they decided afterward to bring this experience to others. This concept is now known as "Nightfever", and it is bearing good fruit all over the world. During a Nightfever, there are eight to ten priests sitting in the side aisles of a church. In front of each priest, there is a lit candle and a sign indicating what he has to offer: "Conversation", "Blessing", "The Sacrament of Reconciliation". Long lines quickly form in front of these signs. Why? Because in confession, we receive the liberating power of God's forgiveness and start anew with God. The joy that is experienced by the person receiving forgiveness can really be seen. At one Nightfever, a visitor saw how a young woman walked away from confession completely freed and happy. The visitor could sense the weight that had been lifted from the woman's shoulders. So, the visitor approached me and said: "That's what I want, too." She didn't know exactly how to make a confession, but she had seen what happens when you do. That's why I can recommend to you with all my heart:

Make a new start! Go to confession!

Fr. Andreas Süss
Spiritual Director of Nightfever

1. GO TO CONFESSION!

Why It's Great to Seek Reconciliation with God and How to Do It

Bernhard Meuser

What tops the list of things people like doing least? Going to the dentist, of course. But for most, going to confession is a close second.

What? Tell a complete stranger the worst things about myself? Do you think I'm crazy?! Go to a priest and tell him that I have stolen, cheated, and lied, or that I wanted the person next to me at school to go to hell or that I have been surfing awful pages on the Internet? No way! What would he think of me? I wouldn't be able to look him in the eye again!

Sure, sometimes you need a lot of courage to be able to face the dark side of your life.

We all want to be the greatest in some way.

We want to shine. We want to be admired, and there is truly a lot to admire in us.

- One's a math whiz
- The other's amazing at sports
- Still another is such a good friend he would give you the shirt off his back if you needed it

But we all know we do wrong.

We can try to hide our dark side for a while. But one day it is going to come out that my brilliant essay is all "copy & paste". When we lie, we get found out: "So you've been lying to me for years!" Then we have to admit that the bad habit has us in its grip. That's painful.

Cowards then try to explain themselves and make excuses. But the brave say:

"Yes, I admit it.
I have really
messed
up.
Please forgive me!"

In most cases, having the courage to confess pays off. But often we are left with an empty feeling. I once had to speak these difficult words to a friend: "Can you forgive me again?" What did my friend say? "Okay, I can forgive you, but I can never forget!" *Hey*, I thought, *what kind of forgiveness is that?!* But I replied, "Then I would rather you forget it than forgive me."

Hello, God, I'm still here!

I went to confession again a few days ago. Hello, God, I'm still here! I've messed up pretty badly. I've turned away from you.

I know exactly why I need to confess. Every sin, every lack of kindness offends YOU. You alone are God! Only you can forgive me.

Here I am, please forgive me!

Although I have been to confession many times in my life, I still have to push myself to go, even though I also know that within five minutes of leaving the confessional, I feel as happy as I do after a swim in the sea.

- There is peace in my soul.
- I could sing and dance for joy.
- Not everyone experiences such a spontaneous joy, but that's how it is for me.

Okay, I wanted to tell you about this special confession. After I had confessed my sins, the priest said a few words to me that soothed my soul like a balm: "When I absolve you of your sins in the name of Jesus, you really can start anew. Just imagine. Totally new! Yes, you begin life again from scratch. And I'll tell you something else:

God, who is Love, doesn't just *forgive* your sins— in a certain sense, he even *forgets* them!"

Wow! I could have given the man a hug!

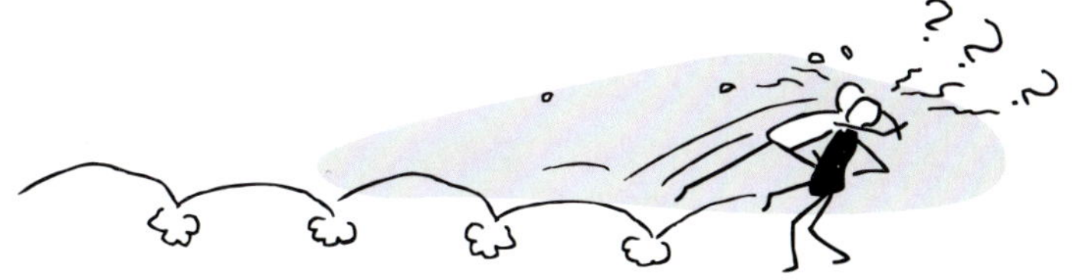

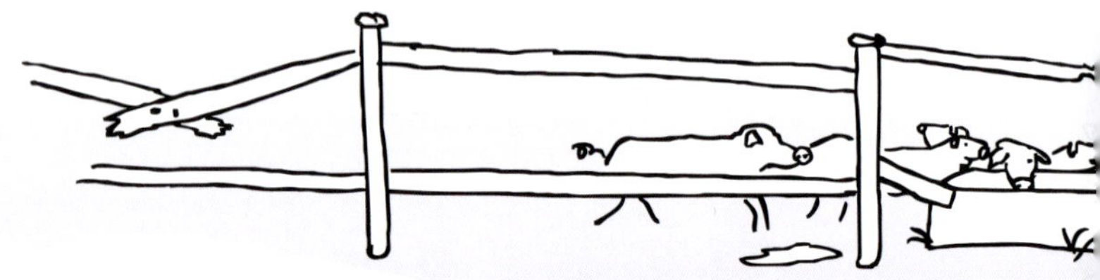

What's God like? Simply awesome!

Yes, I often think about this myself. Hey, God, how did I deserve your being so interested in me?! You know what I'm like! I really don't have much to show for my life.

But clearly my smallness doesn't matter to God. His love is steadfast. And what does that make me do? I surrender. I come back like the prodigal son in the Gospel. Sometimes I just can't believe how our Father in heaven once again stretches out his arms and welcomes me with joy. I stammer like the prodigal son: "Father, I have sinned against heaven and before you; I am no longer worthy to be called your son!" (Lk 15:21).

I just can't believe how God responds to me, the repentant sinner. Normally, you would think, "That's the end of me. His accusing look is going to destroy me! Shouldn't he say something like 'Stop it! Get out of my sight! I don't want to *ever, ever, ever* see you again!'?"

But that's exactly what God doesn't do! He is utterly happy that I have found my way back to him. He has even prepared a feast for me. The best of everything!

Many people say, "I've done so many bad things that God couldn't possibly forgive me." This is blasphemy. It means putting limits on God's mercy. But his mercy has no limits: it is boundless. Nothing offends the good Lord more than doubting his mercy.

SAINT JOHN VIANNEY (CURÉ OF ARS)

What is confession?

+ Confession is like performing **a regular**

update

on my life. If I miss the update, then all my software is out-of-date. My laptop is unprotected and exposed to viruses and trojan attacks.

+ Confession is like **taking in a car for**

service.

At least every 10,000 miles, the car needs to go to the mechanic. Otherwise, it will eventually stop working and the engine will break down. At least once a year—preferably before Easter—every Catholic should go to confession.

+ Confession is like **taking a**

shower

after an intense walk. You come home—dead tired. The dust from the road sticks to your skin. You stink, and there's no way you can be around others in this state. But after a shower, you feel like a new person. Your skin can breathe again. You feel alive again. You put on fresh clothes.

+ Confession is like **getting**

back on track.

Sinning is like driving 100 miles per hour on the wrong side of the road. If you want to avoid a crash, you have only one choice: get back on the right side of the road! (And slow down.)

Perhaps you can think of other comparisons?

! Perhaps you want to know just what exactly is not going well (or is going completely wrong) in your life. Work carefully through the following pages. They're all about examining your conscience.

2. IN & OUT

A Different Kind of Confession Guide

If you want to examine your conscience—at the end of the day, on holiday, or because you want to go to confession now—a confession guide can often help. Of course, nothing surpasses the Ten Commandments and the Lord's Commandment to love God and neighbor. You can find them at the back of this book. You can also find a detailed confession guide in the YOUCAT.

Here is a confession guide in the form of an **IN & OUT** list. It provides a few pointers on what to let *in* your life and what to keep *out*. The most important word in this guide is "love". Love is always essential. Without love, everything falls apart: society, family, your own life. Whoever truly loves is on the direct way to God, who is Love.

This **IN & OUT** list is not just a guide that lists various sins. Instead, under *In*, you will find things that really make us happy. Keep in mind that loving, passionately seeking the good, and improving daily are a thousand times more helpful than constantly fixating on faults for fear of making tiny mistakes (this behavior is under *Out*). You should be, above all, a person who loves much. Keep in mind that this is not at all a complete list, but only a guide to get you started.

LO

FOR GOD

IN

Giving God the first place in your life

Giving witness as a Christian

Keeping a crucifix, an icon, a biblical poster, a sign of your faith in your room

Thinking about God first thing in the morning and last thing at night

Going to Mass on Sundays

Defending God when others trash him

Calling on God, asking him to come into your life

Looking for God and his will in the Bible and in the Church

Informing yourself about your faith, educating yourself

Examining your conscience every day, going to confession regularly

OUT

Postponing your relationship with God until later

Considering yourself the greatest

Loving someone or something more than God

"Taking a break" from God on vacation

Superstitions, witchcraft, Tarot, astrology

Escaping through distractions, having no time for God

Being ashamed of one's faith

Blaspheming against God, swearing, challenging him

Spreading gossip about the Church without checking the facts

Comparing yourself to other people and thinking yourself better or worse than they are

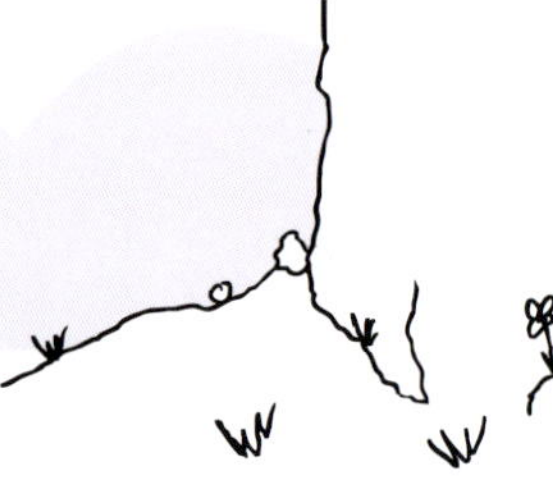

VE

FOR THE WORLD

IN

Enjoying life

Thanking God for what's beautiful as well as for what's difficult in life

Getting involved in politics, in society, in your church. Taking responsibility for others.

Being aware, carefully reading and watching the news, thoughtfully writing letters to the editor

Singing, dancing, playing sports

Cooking something special and sharing it with others

Going out into nature

Making the world more of a home

Marveling at creation, gazing in wonder at the stars in heaven

Listening to music and making music yourself

OUT

Living purely for your own pleasure

Leaving the world to its own fate

Eating only junk food and producing unnecessary waste

Working only for your own bank account

Not resisting greed

Spoiling the environment

Being cruel to animals

Exploiting the land and the labor and love of others; abusing the human body

Hiding, burying your talents and gifts

Being lazy, letting things fall apart

Whining, criticizing everything, being pessimistic

FOR OTHERS

IN

Being grateful

Forgiving others from the heart and asking for forgiveness yourself

Making others happy

Patiently accepting those who are difficult

Acting nobly, being honorable and idealistic

Praying for others

Calling injustice by its name

Helping older people and people with disabilities

Rejoicing with others, having compassion for others

Sticking up for outsiders

Treating people with respect

Being honest, without hurting others

Being 100% faithful

OUT

Being malicious, gossiping, tearing others down

Stealing books, films, or music off the Internet

Deceiving, tricking, lying, being false

Manipulating others, using others for your own ends

Spreading others' secrets

Looking down on others

Leading someone astray, using someone sexually

Envying others

Saying nothing when your friends do drugs

Making false promises

Being unforgiving, not wanting to recognize your own mistakes

Endangering others on the road

Assisting in or agreeing to an abortion

FOR MYSELF

IN

Growing in faith, building a true relationship with God

Never ceasing to work on yourself, educating yourself, becoming a better person

Recognizing your own strengths/weaknesses

Accepting yourself as God accepts you, looking at yourself in a positive light

Looking after your body with care, with sun, fresh air, and exercise

Waiting until marriage

Being able to laugh at yourself, not taking yourself too seriously

Forgiving yourself

Enjoying food

Not complaining about everything

Discerning what's important and what's not

Taking care of your conscience

OUT

Neglecting symptoms, not going to the doctor

Being fanatical about the way you look

Smoking, taking drugs, getting drunk

Viewing pornography, masturbating

Making everything subordinate to your career

Looking for pity

Sex before marriage, homosexual acts, gender transitioning

Abusing your body, overworking to an extreme

Carelessly putting your life at risk

Being selfish

Letting yourself be ruled by bad habits

THE SACRAMENT OF PENANCE and RECONCILIATION

(Commonly Known as Confession)

How Does It Work?
What Do You Need?
How Do You Do It?

First of all, you need

contrition.

This means really being sorry and trying not to sin again. It's not enough simply to mumble something with your lips just because you read somewhere that this or that is a sin.

You need to be convinced that you have done something wrong, that you have hurt or sullied yourself or others, that you have turned away from God and messed up the divine order. Your conscience is left hanging when it is not oriented toward God's commandments. (You can find the Ten Commandments and the Lord's Commandment at the end of this book.) Before examining your conscience, you need to know, for example, "You shall not lie" (Eighth Commandment).

But be careful. We like to deceive ourselves and say, "Hey, I'll decide that with my conscience! I'll answer for that myself!"

→ 1 Jn 1:8

People have lied, betrayed, and murdered after consulting their own consciences. So, if you are unsure about anything, ask your priest. He can help you to check your conscience against God's commandments.

→ 297

Can a person form his conscience?

For contrition, you also need

resolution.

> Resolution is the first step toward a real act. I must take concrete measures.
>
> ADRIENNE VON SPEYR

This means you must genuinely have the intention not to recommit the sins that you confess to the priest.

Now, you might say, "That's impossible! I know full well that I'll turn to drugs again. I just won't manage without them." That's you thinking you're being realistic. It's true you might not manage immediately to say goodbye to drugs forever. But if you really have the intention to do so and really want to give it your best shot, you can be sure that God will grant you forgiveness and peace through the ministry of the priest. You will see. In confession, you receive a supernatural power for goodness that we call "grace". Perhaps afterward you will be overcome by the urge to do wrong and won't resist the temptation, even though you hate it. Simply go back to confession again. You can go back a thousand times with the same story. It won't stop God's mercy, not one bit.

→ Lk 15:11–32

God is always the Father with open arms, and he is always preparing a feast for you. Don't believe me? It's true!

Then you will also need to

confess.

This means that it's not enough to collect your sins and omissions in your heart and to beam them up quickly once a week before falling asleep. You need the Church.

It's very important to make a small examination of conscience regularly. But if you really want to be fully reconciled with God (or need to be because you have committed a grave sin that is separating you from God), the only thing that helps is confessing to a priest.

→ **Jn 20:23**

Jesus gave the apostles and their followers an almost unbelievable power when he said, "If you forgive the sins of any, they are forgiven; if you retain the sins of any, they are retained." Only God can forgive sins. Jesus Christ entrusts this power to the Church. God's love wanted things to be concrete. If you really want to start again in your life, you shouldn't just phone self-reproaches up to heaven. Go to a priest, and say, "This is how it is. I committed this sin so many times. I repent before God." If the priest sees that you really mean it, he will grant you God's forgiveness.

→ **228** Who can forgive sins?

! Read more about "serious" sins (pp. 81–82) and the power to forgive sins (p. 73) in Supplement II: Tough Questions on Confession

COME RIGHT IN!

Or, The Rite of Confession

Let's just assume you opted for the confessional rather than a face-to-face confession.* You examined your conscience beforehand, and maybe you also wrote some notes for yourself.** You asked God the Holy Spirit to grant you a good confession.*** Okay, then! The green light outside the confessional is on (or there's another sign indicating that no one else is confessing at that moment). So you go in.

The priest greets you. Now it's your turn. You make the Sign of the Cross, saying:

In the name of the Father and of the Son and of the Holy Spirit. Amen.

The priest then says the following or similar words:

May God, who has enlightened every heart, help you to know your sins and trust in his mercy.

To which you reply:

Amen.

Easy!

You now have time to confess your sins, time to "accuse yourself". It sounds harsh, but that's exactly what it means. You should confess your guilt, not state your innocence. So, it's a proper personal accusation. Wow, that takes courage.

Simply say what realizations you had after examining your life before God. There are two fundamental questions to ask yourself, both equally important. The first is:

What **wrong** have I **done**?

And the second is:

What **good** have I **failed to do**?

Here's a small tip, just in case you can't think of how you've sinned. Sometimes we sin more by what we don't do than by what we do.

You can take your confession notes** with you if it helps.

At the end of your confession, you should say something that expresses your contrition. For example:

These are my sins.
I acknowledge them humbly and with remorse.

* See Supplement I: Behind the Screen or Face-to-Face? (p. 68).
** Find out more on page 51.
*** Take a look at a few prayers for confession beginning on page 35.

Now it's the priest's turn!

He may ask you a question, but he'll do so with great care and courtesy. The priest isn't trying to catch you out. It is *your* confession, and the confessor is offering you a divine ministry. He wants to help you to acknowledge your sins and put them into words.

He then gives you some spiritual advice, which means he says things to you that may help you.

The priest then gives you a small penance, which is usually a prayer to be said after confession. This represents a small sign of your

repentance

and your intention to

make reparation

for having offended God with your sin. This reparation is a component of the sacrament of penance. It means repairing as far as possible any damage you have caused to yourself and others. If you have stolen something, you need to give it back (even if you do so anonymously). If you have hurt someone, you need at least to apologize to them.

That's when the priest can grant you

absolution.

God, the Father of mercies,
through the death and resurrection of his Son
has reconciled the world to himself
and poured out the Holy Spirit
for the forgiveness of sins;
through the ministry of the Church
may God grant you pardon and peace.
And I absolve you from your sins
in the name of the Father, and of the Son,
+ and of the Holy Spirit.

Your response is: *Amen.*

To conclude, the priest says:

The Lord has freed you from your sins. Go in peace.

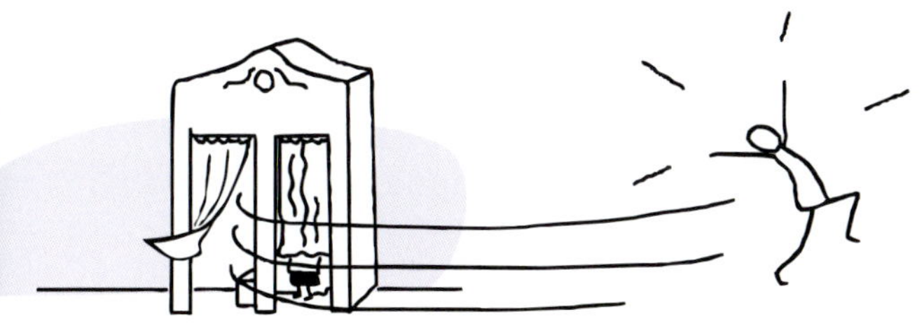

GOOD PRAYERS FOR CONFESSION

Many people think that prayer is pretty much talking to yourself. Not true. You are talking to God. If it helps, light a candle and gaze at a crucifix or an icon. In dialogue with God, a great deal becomes clear to you about yourself. A good confession is always accompanied by good prayers. You may want to pray using your own words, or you may want to use these prayers:

Wash me thoroughly from my iniquity,

And cleanse me from my sin!
For I know my transgressions,
and my sin is ever before me.
Against you, you only, have I sinned,
and done that which is evil in your sight.
Wash me, and I shall be whiter than snow.
Make me hear joy and gladness;
let the bones which you have broken rejoice.
Cast me not away from your presence,
and take not your Holy Spirit from me.
Restore to me the joy of your salvation,
and uphold me with a willing spirit.
Amen.

PSALM 51

A prayer for a good examination of conscience

Come, O my dear Lord,

and teach me in like manner.

And, for that end, give me, O my Lord,
that purity of conscience
which alone can receive,
which alone can improve Thy inspirations.
My ears are dull,
so that I cannot hear Thy voice.
My eyes are dim,
so that I cannot see Thy tokens.
Thou alone canst quicken my hearing,
and purge my sight,
and cleanse and renew my heart.
Teach me, like Mary, to sit at Thy feet,
and to hear Thy word. Amen.

SAINT JOHN HENRY NEWMAN

A prayer to the Holy Spirit for a good confession

Come, Holy Spirit,

Give me the grace to recognize my sins exactly
that I may truly repent of them,
that I may confess them honestly and sincerely
and genuinely improve. Amen.

Acts of contrition

O my God,

I am truly sorry
that I have responded so poorly
to your love for me.
It hurts deep within my soul
that I have sinned
in my words,
my thoughts, my actions and omissions
against your never-ending mercy.
Forgive me, Lord.
Look kindly on me as I come to you,
imperfect and with empty hands.
Have mercy on me.
I believe that you want to welcome me
back as your child.
I seek your love and your boundless forgiveness.
I firmly resolve to do penance,
not to sin again,
and to avoid the near occasions of sin.
Cure me
through your suffering and death,
and give me the grace
to respond better to your love.
Amen.

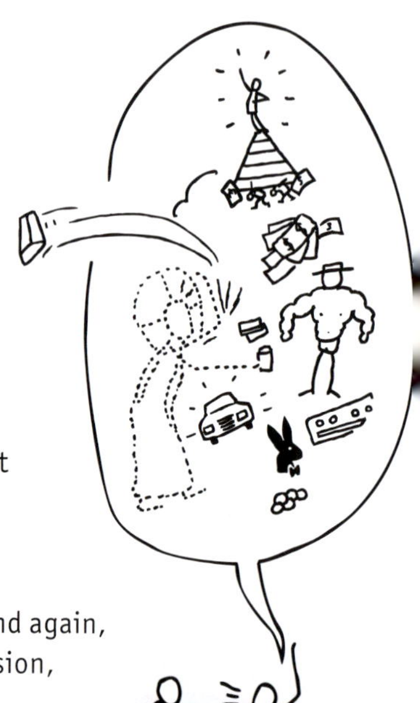

Jesus,

I'm sorry
that I failed again to love you.
The temptation was often so great
and I myself too weak
or my trust in you too small.
I thank you
for wanting to forgive me again and again,
and, strengthened by this confession,
I promise to take up once again
the challenge to live a new life,
a life that pleases you.

I ask you to give me strength for all the battles
that await me, and to make me aware
that you are always with me.
I am happy that you count on me
and still have so much planned for me.
Let me not be discouraged, my God,
by the disappointments
that I cause you.
Amen.

RUDOLF GEHRIG

How beautiful

it is, good Father,
that we cannot fall from your hands.
They are beneath us when we fall;
they are beside us when we waver;
they are above us in danger.

BERNHARD MEUSER

Oh God,

when I stumble over all the hurdles
and fall in every trial
and collapse in every situation
and finally am out for the count
and fail to get up,
there you are at the bottom of the pit—
with me and my faith.

BERNHARD MEUSER

Most merciful redeemer,

may I know you more clearly,
love you more dearly,
and follow you more nearly, day by day.

SAINT RICHARD OF CHICHESTER

My Lord and My God,

take from me everything that keeps me from You. My Lord and my God, give to me everything that brings me near to You. My Lord and my God, take me away from myself and give me entirely to You.

SAINT NICHOLAS OF FLÜE

Father,

I abandon myself into your hands. Do with me what you will. Whatever you may do, I thank you: I am ready for all, I accept all. Let only your will be done in me and in all your creatures—I wish no more than this, O Lord. Into your hands I commend my soul: I offer it to you with all the love of my heart, for I love you, Lord, and so need to give myself, to surrender myself into your hands without reserve and with boundless confidence, for you are my Father.

SAINT CHARLES DE FOUCAULD

recon-

3.

CONFESS? YES, I CAN!

Rudolf Gehrig, nineteen, had graduated from high school. He was volunteering in the parish of Senden, in Germany, to discern what God wanted for his life. Confession became an important part of his life after he attended a World Youth Day.

It was only meant to be a simple prank. I fired one of those large rubber bands across the classroom, but it hit the glass on the door, then landed right in the teacher's face. I was consequently reprimanded and had to go through the school playground at every break time picking up trash with tongs and dropping it in a big garbage bag. Great!! Do you have any idea how much bubble gum a playground of that size holds? Well, I do. Anyway, one break wasn't enough to clean up the whole playground, and even the places that I had cleaned up were just as bad again the following day.

Too much trash in my life

A banana peel can take approximately one year to decompose, depending on the condition of the soil and the level of humidity. A plastic bag can take between 1,000 and 3,000 years, and uranium-238 reduces to only half its size after 4.5 billion years. Yet that's nothing compared to the trash that never decomposes—sin. At a certain point in my life, I understood that sin produces a particular type of trash that can be classified as "highly toxic" because it affects everyone and influences—even destroys—our lives. It

makes my inner landscape filthy. Sin has no half-life; it doesn't break down. But there is a way of getting rid of all this garbage—through confession.

Start again!

Whenever our hearts condemn us . . . God is greater than our hearts, and he knows everything.
1 JOHN 3:20

→ 314

How do we know that God is merciful?

Confession is really quite simple. This much I know. God says to me, "Yes, you have sinned, but because you are truly sorry and because I love you, I forgive you." He throws out all my debts, presses the Reset button, empties the Recycle Bin, and clicks Restart, giving me another opportunity to make a new beginning.

Yet I don't at all go "right back to the beginning". It's not like in the board game "Sorry!", where the little figure has to go straight back to the first tile and make the whole journey again. It's more like a toy-car racetrack. I start going off track because of all the sins that have built up over time. God takes my car and puts it back on the racetrack. I don't have to go right back to the beginning. I just carry on from where I went off. I'm back in the race again, all cleaned up with a full tank. Hey, from now on I'm driving with a new set of tires.

It's not what I want, but it just keeps happening

Ever since the Fall of Adam and Eve, well, that's just the way it is. The thing with sin is that it tends to keep happening in one form or another no matter how hard I try to fight it. If I ever got to the point where I could say, "Yes! I've made it. I know I'll never sin again", I would either be dead or so blinded by arrogance that it would really be high time I went to confession.

→ 68

Original sin? What does the Fall of Adam and Eve have to do with us?

How was your day?

Every evening before I go to sleep, I get into a conversation with God. God asks me, "Hey, son, what good did you do today? Where did you mess up?" That way I prevent certain sins from becoming a habit and my conscience from slowly going numb. C. S. Lewis once compared the conscience to a sharp stone in the heart. The stone pierces your heart each time you sin. But if you sin over and over, so that the stone is constantly touching the wall of the heart, your heart eventually forms such a callus that you don't even notice you are sinning.

The door of Penance means for us that we let our eyes be opened.
JOSEPH RATZINGER (BENEDICT XVI)

I need an early warning system

With some things, I know immediately when I am on the wrong track. With others, I don't realize it. But here, too, the priest to whom I confess (my confessor) has helped me on more than one occasion to see clearly. I have also learned a lot through reading the Holy Scriptures or flipping through the *Catechism*.

→ 312
How does a person know that he has sinned?

I have seen how easily I can end up on the wrong track. Here is an example:

I hit my little brother. I really hadn't meant to. He's normally a nice kid. So what happened? Well, there was this thing with two dollars that were lying on my desk and suddenly disappeared. My brother denied it and emptied his piggy bank to prove he hadn't taken the money. Still, I'm not too convinced of his innocence. Then he took the last bread roll at breakfast even though I was still really hungry but had held back out of courtesy to see if Mom or Dad

” Love begins today. Today someone is suffering. Today someone is on the streets. Today someone is hungry. Today we have to commit. Yesterday is gone. Tomorrow has not yet come. We only have today to make God known by loving, serving, feeding the hungry, clothing the naked, finding shelter for the poor. Don't wait until tomorrow! They will be dead tomorrow if we don't give them something today.

SAINT MOTHER TERESA OF CALCUTTA

wanted it. My little brother gets away with everything. They never tell him off. It hurt me to watch how he showed our parents the picture he'd painted, all proud, and how Mom stuck it straight on the fridge door. Then he came into my room three times without knocking, and when I caught him with my cell phone after he had looked at all my text messages, I just hit him. He then went crying to Mom, my hand stung, and I suddenly felt really sorry. I asked myself what got me so annoyed.

Be angry but do not sin; do not let the sun go down on your anger.

EPHESIANS 4:26

I realize it's often the little things that turn into disasters. Having an early warning system helps. I can take precautions and avoid certain occasions for sin. For example, if I know it's better for me not to take my computer into the bedroom, then I leave it outside. This is better than having to kneel before God the next morning and ask him to forgive me because I've been surfing through the murky waters of the Internet until the early hours of the morning.

Do not bargain with any temptation. Courage itself often intimidates temptations.

SAINT FAUSTINA KOWALSKA

I have to want it, too!

A friend of mine who clearly enjoys his food started a real strict diet six weeks before Christmas and managed to keep it up for five weeks. Then a package arrived from his aunt. It sat on the table for a while, unopened. He knew exactly what was inside—a whole batch of home-baked cookies. My friend knew that as soon as he unwrapped the package and saw those cookies, he'd lose all self-control and scarf the whole thing down. He took another look. He suddenly opened it, and then it was too late—the diet was over.

> Do what you can, and ask his aid in what you cannot do.
>
> SAINT AUGUSTINE

It's no use having an early warning system if my will is weak. To resist the destructive power of sin in my life, I need not only understanding but a healthy dose of *willpower*—and obviously a sound judgment, discerning good from evil.

→ **291**
How can a person tell whether his action is good or bad?

A little plug for "confession notes"

Yeah, yeah. I know you shouldn't have to write down your sins if you want to go to confession. No one who regularly receives the sacrament of reconciliation with God does that. Well, someone once said to me: "Confession notes and a confession guide are like the left and right crutches for a good confession. Once you've learned how to walk you can throw them out." But hey, I haven't gotten that far yet! I'll keep using both for as long as I need to. I want to take my relationship with God very seriously.

A confession guide really helps me. Without it, I remember only that I haven't killed anyone or robbed a bank, which is already a start. I need "the list" to remind me that it's not just about the *bad* things that I *did* do, but just as much about the things I've really messed up—the *good* things that I failed to do for God, for others, and for myself.

> Our dear Lord loves being interrupted.
>
> SAINT JOHN VIANNEY (CURÉ OF ARS)

Working on my list of faults

> ” Cease to lament for that thou canst not help/ And study help for that which thou lament'st.
>
> WILLIAM SHAKESPEARE

I use a confession guide because I'm still "in training". I go through it point by point the same way that train inspectors use a checklist to inspect high-speed train cars. I carry over the relevant points to my "list of faults". The feeling of shock that I get when I reach the end of a long list of faults is already the "contrition" I need if I want God to forgive my sins. The "tough nuts" are at the top of my list so that I can get them out of the way quickly at confession and am not tempted to leave them out because I feel embarrassed.

> ” To recognize the will of God, you need three things: prayer, patience, and counsel.
>
> SAINT JOHN BOSCO

Rip! Rip! Rip!

The thing with the confession list is that it has a special symbolic function. Once it has served its purpose, I tear it up into tiny little pieces—rip, rip, rip.

It's as if everything that stood between me and God has been blown away. Just read what Paul wrote in his letter to the Colossians. Christ has "canceled the bond which stood against us" (Col 2:14).

→ Col 2:13–14

One other thing. I don't share my confession list by text, post it on Facebook, or scribble it in my math notebook. I simply take some paper and write it—the day before the confession at the earliest. Immediately after absolution, all that should remain are tiny scraps blown away by the wind. (That's only a metaphor. Don't litter!)

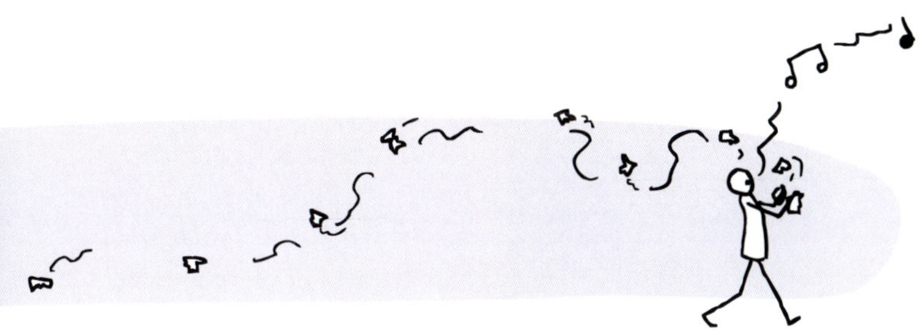

STOP!

What matters most is love!

Some people overdo it when they examine their conscience. Their Christian life and their prayer life consist in frantically looking for new sins that they might have committed. They think God will love them only if they make themselves as small and as bad as they can in front of him. They stop living life to the full. They don't dare to do anything, lest they make a mistake. Instead of praising God's greatness, all they can think about are their own weaknesses. They're constantly telling God what terrible sinners they are.

These people are called *scrupulous* ("scruples" = false inhibitions). A well-known confessor, the French Curé of Ars, John Vianney (1786–1859), often had to deal with the scrupulous. Anyone who went to him for confession had to avoid "all pointless self-accusations, all those scruples repeated over that waste the confessor's time and annoy everyone waiting at the confessional".

The Curé of Ars recommended confessing what was uncertain as uncertain and what was certain as certain. What mattered to him was "that nothing should be false. Speak from the heart. You might be able to fool your confessor, but you can never fool our dear Lord."

It's clear that people need to make an examination of conscience time and again. But please, keep it *short, clear, and to the point!* The Curé of Ars preferred short, honest, succinct confessions.

- God forgives and "forgets" sins.
- So you need to forget them, too.
- Stop fixating on the sin.
- Look at God who is Love.

Christians should be recognized by their joy.

God doesn't want you to walk around like depressed people who continually look into the abyss of their own souls.

BERNHARD MEUSER

I'm looking for a priest

I know that many people would rather get rid of their sins by praying to Jesus on their own or pouring out their hearts to their best friend and then being forgiven automatically. However, Jesus gave the Church the authority to forgive sins. Jesus makes the rules of the game. Believing him, I seek out a priest so that I can start fresh. Although you can't go to the laundromat after it's closed, you can always go to a priest. Of course, this privilege shouldn't be abused. But in the case of an emergency, as when someone is dying in the middle of the night and needs to confess, you should not hesitate to call a priest. Every parish has its own times for confession. I can look them up on the Internet or in the parish newsletter, or else just ask the parish priest.

→ 228
Who can forgive sins?

I have asked myself whether it's better to confess to a priest I know well or to go to someone who doesn't know me at all. I do both, but I somewhat prefer the second option.

→ 238
May a priest later repeat something he has learned in confession? [Spoiler alert: No.]

How often do I go to confession? The rule is clear to me. Anyone who

has committed a serious sin should go to confession and may not receive Communion until doing so. The rule is that every Catholic must go to confession at least once a year. In fact, the Church strongly recommends more regular confession, even for venial sins. How often do I go myself? A few times a year. I really ought to go more often.

! Confession behind the screen or face-to-face confession—what's better? (see p. 68)

→ **234**
When is a Catholic obliged to confess his serious sins? How often should one go to confession?

Don't get hung up on it!

I can suddenly think of a thousand reasons not to keep my appointment with HIM in the confessional. I suddenly remember that I need to clean out the rabbit hutch or that I haven't called my friend back or that the carburetor on my motorcycle badly needs replacing. Or I suddenly decide that I'm not as bad as I thought, that my sins are my business, not my priest's, and that I'm embarrassed to have ever believed in this nonsense about forgiveness of sins. Okay, I don't want to shrug off my responsibility here, but it bears saying that there is someone at work on the other side who really doesn't like me to be reconciled with God. Shot nerves, sweating, racing heart, high blood pressure, bladder problems? Off to the doctor! Or off to the confessional. It's now or never!

> Remember that before you reach the Promised Land, you have to cross the Red Sea and the desert.
>
> SAINT JOHN BOSCO

Before I rush into the confessional, I take a minute to speak with God. Once I'm in the confessional and the door's shut behind me, my heart

! You can find good prayers to prepare for confession on pages 35 to 41.

seems to beat faster than it did on my first date. No wonder. After all, I am meeting someone more powerful and impressive than anyone else on this earth! The priest is there on behalf of Christ himself.

The priest is only "the ear"

After the introduction, off I go. I just say everything! I work through my confession list, point by point. Sometimes I just use my list as a prompt. The priest listens to me in Jesus' place. He is "the ear", everything else is secondary. I am speaking to Jesus. He knows me, and he is not surprised when I pull out from the corner of my heart another bag of garbage I had almost forgotten about. He also knows about the dark parts of my soul, and he is pleased that I am finally letting in light. Once I have told Jesus my sins, I make an act of contrition. It's nothing complicated. It simply means that I add an "I'm sorry" to the "I broke the window." It's enough to say, "Those are my sins. I acknowledge them and am sorry."

! Details of how to make a confession can be found on pages 30 to 33.

→ 232 What must I bring to a confession?

It took me a while to understand that God knows I am a weak creature and yet loves me anyway. There's no need for me to put on a look of innocence to soften his heart or pacify him. My sins offend and disappoint God, but he is pleased whenever I am wholeheartedly sorry and ask him for forgiveness. Contrition is so important. Without it, I might as well not go to confession.

In the whole history of mankind, God has never turned away anyone who has asked for forgiveness. Not exactly an obvious fact, when you think about how you would react if, for example, your friend kept making a mess of everything. He apologizes, you forgive him, he does it again. At a certain point, anybody would be fed up.

Not God.

" Forgiveness is not an occasional act; it is a permanent attitude.

MARTIN LUTHER KING, JR.

→ 314

How do we know that God is merciful?

" For those who love God, he changes everything into good. He even allows our faults and mistakes to be changed into good.

SAINT AUGUSTINE

It's already been paid

Just imagine. I'm standing in the bank with a list of debts. I go to the counter. A nice man with a smart tie is sitting there. My whole body shakes while he goes through my debts. Then I confess to him that, regrettably, I can't pay off any of them. I'm at the end of my resources. What does he do, the man at the counter? He looks up, gazes kindly into my eyes, then rips up my list of debts into tiny pieces. "It doesn't matter," he says, "it's already been paid."

> God is more prepared to forgive a contrite sinner than a mother is to save her child from a fire.
>
> SAINT JOHN VIANNEY (CURÉ OF ARS)

→ **Eph 2:8–9**

That's how confession works. "It's already been paid." Jesus has paid for me! Yes, it is hard to understand, but two thousand years ago God actually decided to pay for our sins. When a company pays for a team's soccer jerseys, the company boss will naturally expect the players to wear the company logo on their shirts to increase the company's profile and profits. God thinks differently. He pays out of love. God is Love, and love doesn't keep count or seek its own interests.

→ **337**
How are we saved?

Though your sins are like scarlet, they shall be white as snow; though they are red like crimson, they shall become like wool.

ISAIAH 1:18

The priest is the man at the counter of life, ready to tear up my list of debts on God's behalf. It is sad to see how many people run around in despair, using the wildest methods and the most absurd "miracle cures" to get rid of their list of debts instead of just going to the man at the counter and letting him tear it up.

Another great story

> Jesus in the confessional is not a dry cleaner. Confession is an encounter with Jesus. He is waiting for us, and waiting for us just as we are.
>
> POPE FRANCIS

I once heard this cool story. There was a man who had been through a lot in his life and had totally distanced himself from God. One day for "fun", he decided to go to confession and play a joke on the priest. He told him all his wild stories and then, at the end of it all, declared scornfully he wasn't a bit sorry and made fun of the priest's apparent naïveté.

The priest couldn't absolve him of his sins, of course, but he said to the young man, "If you really feel that way, go to the crypt and stand in front of the crucifix. Then look at Jesus and say ten times out loud, 'I don't care that you died for me.'" Struck by his dignity, the man did indeed follow the priest's instructions. He went into the crypt, stood in front of the crucifix, and said, "I don't care that you died for me." He repeated the phrase a few more times. Suddenly

he broke down in tears and threw himself to the ground. He went back once again into the confessional. This time he made a proper confession, and this time he was absolved of his sins and was converted from then on. He had been touched by the love of God.

The priest is only God's tool. He couldn't absolve the young man of his past at first because it was clear that he felt no remorse for his sins. To be truly remorseful, you need to want to avoid sin and change your behavior. Of course, it is difficult to change your behavior and completely refrain from doing wrong in the future. But I should at least try. God will help me. After the absolution, you receive a penance from the priest, usually a prayer. Many people think of "penance" as a kind of gruesome punishment that the Church has devised to intimidate the people. It's more about giving God *a sign of reparation and gratitude* that shows my willingness to make up for the damage done.

" There is no moment in our life when we can't beat a new path.

CHARLES DE FOUCAULD

→ 230
What is penance?

I once went to confession with a priest from South Tirol, and we were having such a good chat that he forgot in the end what penance he was going to give me. He gave me quite a shock when he said, "Okay, then, for your penance, please climb Mount Everest on your knees." In the end, thanks be to God, he reduced it to a prayer.

> How do you defeat evil? Accepting God's forgiveness.... It happens every time we go to confession.
>
> POPE FRANCIS

After confession

I feel enormously happy, liberated! There have been moments when I have cried tears of joy after confession. But there have also been moments when I didn't feel anything. Once I asked a priest if I had done something wrong. He said to me, "You haven't done anything wrong. Your confession worked. In the sacrament of reconciliation, it's a question, not of *feeling* that your sins have been forgiven, but of *knowing* that they have been forgiven. If you also feel something after confession, that's even better!" Phew. That was such a relief.

→ 339

What does God's grace do to us?

What if I fall back into my old ways?

I can keep falling flat on my face as long as I keep picking myself up again to carry on the fight. In moments of carelessness, I have been caught off guard in the boxing ring with the devil and gotten one right on the nose. If I fall to the ground in those moments, it does not mean the fight is lost. The referee starts counting down, and I get back onto my feet! So it makes absolutely no difference how many times I fall, as long as I love the fight and keep getting up again.

I will win because I believe in God and he believes in me.

And Jesus said [to the adulteress], "Neither do I condemn you; go, and do not sin again."

JOHN 8:11

SUPPLEMENT I

Behind the Screen or Face-to-Face?

What's better?

Both are good

Confession **behind the screen** of the confessional booth allows you to remain largely anonymous. Face-to-face confession may allow the priest to know who is confessing, but the point of confession in both forms is that the priest is representing Christ—not being his "own person".

It's important to know that it makes no difference whether the priest hearing your confession is a saint or someone who is struggling in his own life—at least not when it comes to what he does for you in the sacrament. He could still absolve you of your sins under the authority of Christ even if he were a criminal. Let's be honest. Sometimes, when we're having a deep conversation, we hope the priest will downplay our sins by saying, "Hey, it's not that serious!" Yet it annoys me sometimes when priests say things like this. I am standing before God, and if my conscience is pricking me, I don't want to hear, "Oh, you poor thing. You must have had a terrible childhood!"

I myself normally confess behind the screen, about once a month, usually. I go prepared, and the whole thing doesn't take long—five to seven minutes typically. In those moments when I prefer a more detailed discussion about my life, then the confessional is not the appropriate space. On those occasions, I'll meet with the priest in his office, and once I've shared everything with him, he takes his stole and puts it around his neck—that way he can administer the sacrament of penance—and we close the open discussion with a formal confession.

One potential problem with confession is that it's possible just to rattle off a few sins. You quickly list a couple of standard offenses, make the Sign of the Cross, then go back to your everyday life. For some people, confession behind the screen makes things too impersonal. The advantage of it, however, is that you remain anonymous. But whether you're behind the screen or having a face-to-face confession, what you confess always remains completely confidential.

A friend recently told me a story about a confession in Washington, D.C. He went into a confessional in the

cathedral. A green light indicated that a priest was waiting for the next penitent. It was dark in the confessional, so he couldn't see the priest's face behind the screen. My friend started giving a detailed account of his situation, how long he had been married, how many children he had, what he did for a living, and what was on his mind. Suddenly, a loud, deep voice boomed out of the confessional, "No stories, please. Just confess." That's wonderful advice. I can sympathize with the man of God in Washington. It is better to get straight to the point in confession rather than beat around the bush. If you aren't sure about something or other, ask. The confessional is not a divine information booth or a psychotherapist's couch. It's the place where I meet God through his servants.

Having a **face-to-face confession** is also a wonderful way to feel God's love and mercy. I have a few images in my mind. Every week at the Taizé Community in France, which I have often visited, there is a "night of lights". As evening falls, various religious brothers take their places under the arcades. You can speak with some about your life and your walk with God. Others, wearing stoles, are Catholic priests. You can approach them and ask for confession. There is often a long queue of young people waiting to receive the sacrament of reconciliation. It's downright contagious, almost pulling you in with the thought, *Hey, you really ought to get your life with God back in order*. It's a space full of yearning, peace, and beauty. God is at work here. He changes people in the depths of their hearts.

Of course, this kind of discussion can happen behind the screen as well. It is not unique to face-to-face confession.

A face-to-face confession, however, isn't simply a chat, and the priest isn't simply some nice guy who's easy to talk to. The confession is something sacred and not to be trivialized.

SUPPLEMENT II

Tough Questions on Confession

A Bishop Tells Us What We Need to Know

Archbishop Salvatore Cordileone of San Francisco (b. 1956) has been a priest and a confessor for over forty years. Known by young people in the Bay Area as "ABC", he has studied theology and canon law in Rome, pastored poor Catholics near the Mexican border, and led a massive flock of San Franciscans through the dark days of the COVID pandemic, fighting to ensure Catholics had access to the Eucharist and to the sacrament of confession. Archbishop Cordileone—whose Italian last name means "lion heart"—is deeply respected across the United States for his wisdom, compassion, and Christian courage. In this interview, we asked him many of the questions that people often have about confession but are afraid to ask.

If you had to describe the sacrament of penance in one sentence, what would you say?

It is a gift from God, allowing each one of us to hear Jesus himself say, "Your sins are forgiven. Go in peace."

I see how confession is a gift. But did you say that Jesus—not just the priest—is the one who forgives us?

→ Jn 20:23

In the sacraments, it is *Christ himself* who baptizes, who gives us his Body and Blood in the Eucharist, who marries the couple for life, and so on (*CCC* 1127). This is an ancient teaching of the Church, dating back at least to Saint Leo the Great in the fifth century. Jesus acts through other human beings, but mysteriously, it is always the Lord himself who encounters us here and now—even if the priest is far from perfect.

Why is it important to remember that confession is a sacrament?

Our Catholic Tradition has so many beautiful ceremonies, customs, and rituals, but the sacraments have a particularly special place. In them, it is Christ himself who acts, which means that they always work, no matter how flawed the priest is or how ugly the altarpiece is. When Jesus says at Mass, "This is my Body", the bread truly becomes the Body of Christ. The priest may be a sinner, and my own faith may be very weak. It does not matter for the sacrament. When God speaks, it happens—just as in creation. So it is with confession: if I'm truly repentant, then when I receive absolution, I *know* that God has forgiven me.

→ **193**

Is there some inner logic that unites the sacraments with each other?

How did the sacrament of confession develop in the Church?

When Jesus appeared to the apostles after the Resurrection, he told them, "If you forgive the sins of any, they are forgiven; if you retain the sins of any, they are retained" (Jn 20:23). He gave them the power—and the responsibility—to forgive, but not just with a human mercy. "Whatever you bind on earth shall be bound in heaven," he said, "and whatever you loose on earth shall be loosed in heaven" (Mt 18:18). In other words, the pardon that the apostles give is connected to God himself. Historically, though, it took time for the Church to understand this as the sacrament of confession. It was always understood that baptism washes away our sins, but after a while, the Church also had to deal with the fact that people committed sins after baptism. Some of these sins were very grave and public, such as apostasy (denying faith in Christ during persecution), murder, and adultery. The Church determined, of course, that such sinners could be forgiven, but only if they lived a period of serious public penance, to prove they were committed to change. Later, the focus moved from open scandals that affected the community to the individual's private spiritual journey, the personal search for holiness. Here, both the sins and the forgiveness began to take place in secret. It is important to see, above all, that the Church has always understood this sacrament as *medicine*, a grace given by Christ to make us spiritually whole and help us become saints.

What is the seal of confession, and why does it matter?

The seal of confession is one of the most sacred realities in the Church, and essential to the sacrament itself.

The sacrifice acceptable to God is a broken spirit; a broken and contrite heart, O God, you will not despise.

PSALM 51:17

→ 238

May a priest later repeat something he has learned in confession? [Spoiler alert: No.]

You cannot sin away God's love.

HEINRICH CHRISTIAN RUST

It means that the priest can never, under any circumstances, reveal what has been told to him in confession. This even includes crimes under investigation. Part of the healing brought about in this sacrament comes from my honest admission of what I have done wrong, so that Christ can mend that wound. For this reason, the penitent must know without a doubt that what is revealed in confession is sacrosanct and completely confidential.

People sometimes say that the Church invented confession just to control people. Is this true?

No. The Church did not invent the power to forgive sins. She received this straight from the risen Lord, who on Easter night said to his apostles: "Receive the Holy Spirit. If you forgive the sins of any, they are forgiven" (Jn 20:22–23). Why is this important? Mercy is at the heart of Christ's mission, but with this mercy comes a real conversion of the heart. Sin makes us miserable, and our loving God wants us to have joy—true joy, not short-term, superficial happiness. When we sin, we don't just break a rule; we betray a relationship. Forgiveness goes hand in hand with real change, and the Church takes responsibility for guiding the faithful toward a genuine conversion. Still, Catholics come to confession freely, so any "control" here comes in the form of an encouragement to holiness. Authentic holiness can never be forced.

Why is God so interested in my sins?

Because he sees the awful impact sin has on us. It distorts the divine image and isolates us, bringing us unbelievable pain. Adam and Eve were once happy walking in the garden with God, but what happened after the Fall? They became afraid, paranoid, deeply unhappy. The best proof of how serious sin is, and how much God wants to deliver us from it, is Jesus' sacrifice on the Cross. It took the death of God, so to speak, to free us from the tight grip of darkness. The sacrament of reconciliation is a share in this liberation that Jesus offers, and it is a powerful work of God our Savior.

> The power of evil lives off the cowardice of the good.
>
> SAINT JOHN BOSCO

What if I go to a confessor who knows me? Won't he think badly of me the next time I see him?

Remember that the priest himself goes to confession. He knows that we all struggle with sin, and if anything, he will respect your courage and honesty. Even if he did "think

→ 396
How does a Christian deal with anger?

badly" of you, he is bound never to say a word about your confession outside the sacrament of penance—not even to you. And you should follow this rule too. Both priest and penitent should treat what is shared in confession as a secret. That being said, admitting our sins always takes humility, a swallowing of our pride, which is part of what makes it so powerful.

If I find it really difficult to express a sin, even though it is weighing heavily on my mind, how do I overcome this fear?

The sins you least want to confess are usually the sins you most need to confess. The fear and embarrassment are actually good things in this case. They show that your conscience is working and has alerted you to something wrong. Remember that Christ wants to offer you "pardon and peace" in confession. It will be a great relief to share this burden with someone else, in the healing exchange of confession. The sooner, the better. If you don't know what to say, then begin with, "Father, the most serious matter weighing on my conscience is ..." Your human condition won't shock the confessor, who has likely heard thousands of confessions before and, even if not, knows well his own sins and failings.

What if I am as vague as possible about my sins in confession?

Think about a trip to the doctor's office. A good physician needs to know precise symptoms to provide the best assistance. If you tell him that you "don't feel good", he does not have much to go on, but if you specify that your stomach has been hurting, that gives him at least a start. Likewise, clarity and preparation are essential to a good confession. At the same time, though, you do not need to go into great detail or tell any long stories; just give enough for the priest to be able to guide you. The standard the Church teaches is that you must confess all of the serious sins you committed since your last confession "in kind and in number", that is, name the sins and give an estimate as to about how many times or how often you committed them.

→ 234

When is a Catholic obliged to confess his serious sins? How often should one go to confession?

How should I confess?

Start with an honest examination of your conscience. Many resources are available to help with this, but at the most basic level, Christ teaches us to love God with all our hearts, and our neighbors as ourselves. Ask the Holy Spirit to reveal to you the places and times where you were not loving toward God, your neighbor, or yourself. God will enlighten you, and if you are patient,

→ 233

What sins must be confessed?

you will clearly recognize them. Then go admit them plainly in confession, without going into too much detail and without trying to blame anyone else. Even if others have wronged you—as they probably have—confession is the place where we take full responsibility for our own share in sin.

→ 233

What sins must be confessed?

Should I confess all sins? What should I confess?

→ 234

When is a Catholic obliged to confess his serious sins? How often should one go to confession?

First of all, if I'm conscious of a truly serious sin, what we call "mortal sin", I should bring that to confession as soon as possible. There are many resources in the Church to help you identify these mortal sins. These are the sins that must be confessed in the sacrament before resuming reception of Holy Communion. Other than that, a review of my life should help me recognize smaller sins or faults that still need healing and conversion—what we call "venial sins". Although these venial sins can be confessed, especially when the penitent needs help overcoming them, they can also be cleansed in other ways, such as through acts of penance and charity.

Does God also forgive sins that I haven't confessed?

When we receive absolution, God forgives all our sins, including those we accidentally forget to confess. It is another matter with grave sins I intentionally avoid confessing. This shows either a lack of true sorrow or, perhaps worse, a lack of trust in God's mercy, and it results in the absolution from the priest being invalid (the sins confessed are not forgiven in the sacrament). Do I think I can hide my sin from him? Do I believe that God can't or won't forgive it? There is no sin God does not already see, and there is no sin so serious that he cannot forgive. God delights in his infinite mercy, but we

> Glory is not found in never falling but in always getting up again.
>
> SAINT AUGUSTINE

→ 235
Can I make a confession even if I have not committed any serious sins?

do have to “confess our sins”, as the letter of James tells us (cf. Jas 5:16). Also, if we later remember something we forgot to confess in a previous confession, we should confess it the next time we approach the sacrament.

Does the confessor always have to give absolution?

If the penitent is truly sorry and honestly desires not to commit this sin again, he can receive absolution. There are no other special requirements. But we need to avoid the idea that this sacrament is automatic, like driving through a car wash. Conversion is deeply personal—true growth in friendship with God. Good relationships are never just pure “routine”. For this reason, saints like Padre Pio have sometimes denied penitents absolution, since they could sense that the confession was not genuine. This is extremely rare, but if it happens to you, see it as an invitation to a richer conversion of heart. Pray more, then go back to make a better confession. If you think the priest is being uncharitable, you’re free to find another confessor. But absolution will always be given when you show true “contrition” for your sins: sorrow for having offended God and the intention not to sin again.

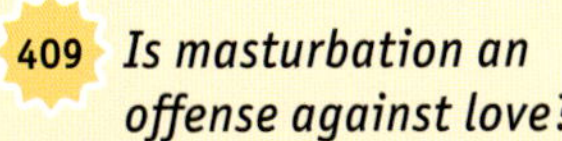

409 *Is masturbation an offense against love?*

[The Church] warns against trivializing it. Many young people and adults are in danger of becoming isolated in their consumption of lewd pictures, films, and Internet services instead of finding love in a personal relationship. Loneliness can lead to a blind alley in which masturbation becomes an addiction. Living by the motto "For sex I do not need anyone; I will have it for myself, however and whenever I need it" makes nobody happy.

After absolution, I still get a penance. Isn't that a punishment?

This term "penance" dates from the early centuries of the Church, when public sinners, such as idolaters, adulterers, and murderers underwent a lengthy period of fasting and exclusion from the Eucharist before being allowed to return to the sacraments. They had to prove they were serious before they could receive Communion and come back into the fold. Our practice now is for the priest to give a "penance" to perform *after* absolution. This practice developed when more frequent confession became common, and confession of less

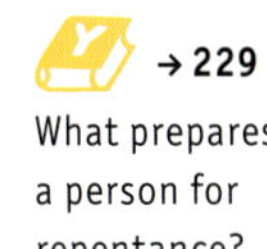
→ 229
What prepares a person for repentance?

serious sins. It is also a reminder that we do not carry out the work of penance *in order to be* forgiven, because God's forgiveness is a pure gift; all he asks for is sincere contrition. Rather, this penance is a realistic step to make the conversion take root. Christ paid the price of our sins on the Cross, a price we could not pay ourselves, but we participate in his self-offering by acts of reparation in the form of works of penance and charity. Just think about when someone makes a supreme sacrifice to rescue you in a moment of distress: let's say you're drowning in the rapids of a river and someone in your hiking group jumps in the water and risks his life to pull you ashore. You can never repay him for the gift of your life, but you nonetheless want to show your thanks with profound gestures of gratitude. This is the human response of love and solidarity. Moreover, although our sin has truly been forgiven, our selfishness has left its mark on us, or on the world around us. The penance is an act of love toward God or neighbor, to counterbalance my selfishness.

Doesn't confession just give me a pass to sin again and then say, "Well, I'll just go and confess everything one more time"?

No. Of course, on the one hand, we can never exhaust God's mercy. He is infinitely patient with us. But going to confession when you *intend* to keep sinning makes no sense, since you lack contrition. To presume on God's

mercy is to abuse God's mercy. However, if you truly want to stop the sin and are simply worried that you will be too weak to resist, this is a different story, because God asks only for your good will.

Why should I confess at all if I am bound to sin again anyway?

If you intend to change, God can make this change happen. To believe otherwise is despair, a lack of hope. It can be a self-fulfilling prophecy, with tragic consequences. I can make a real, firm purpose of amendment, even when I know my own weakness. Frequent confession is a sign that I am honestly striving to do his will, and that is all God asks. And the practice of frequent confession helps you to make progress. It is like the spiritual workout room: just as it takes regular vigorous physical exercise to get into good physical shape, which at first is very difficult but over time because easier and even enjoyable, so regular spiritual exercise helps you to grow in virtue and to desire ever more deeply to please God.

It's so frustrating to confess the same thing every time. What would you say to encourage someone who continues to struggle with the same sin?

Keep struggling! Different temptations bombard us at different times in our lives. Sometimes they are tied to our own personality and history. First of all, give thanks for the areas

→ **Mt 25:40**

in your life that are going well. We often forget that "confession" is also a confession of praise for God's goodness in my life. Secondly, accept with humility the realistic knowledge of where you are likely to fall. Frequent confession, even of the same sins, can be an occasion for spiritual direction.

How often should I go to confession?

→ 235
Can I make a confession even if I have not committed any serious sins?

To most people, I would say, "More often than you go now." If you commit a mortal sin, then run to the confessional. At the same time, we need to avoid scrupulosity, the temptation to go to confession over and over to make sure I'm "really" forgiven. Confession at

regular intervals—at least once a year, but generally once a month for laypeople, or maybe even once a week for some—is like a spiritual checkup, keeping me on track and getting the jump on problems before they become too serious.

You've talked quite a bit about "mortal sin". What is that, exactly?

It is sin that is serious in itself, a direct violation of God's word. The Ten Commandments are the best standard: witchcraft, denying God, slander, murder, adultery, fornication, and so on. It is not mainly a legal problem, though. Mortal sin is a personal rejection of the God who is Love. It "destroys charity in the heart of man" (*CCC* 1855). We see it happen in the story of Adam and Eve, who in effect say to God, "You cannot tell us what is right and wrong. The serpent knows better." The results are disastrous. The classic Catholic criteria for identifying a sin as mortal are (1) the action itself must be a "grave matter", that is, seriously wrong, (2) the person committing it must know it is seriously wrong, and (3) he must choose to do it freely. All three need to hold. A priest can help you discern these, but if you

> ❞ The Sacrament of Reconciliation is *one of the most effective instruments of personal growth*. Here the Good Shepherd, through the presence and voice of the priest, approaches each man and woman, entering into a personal dialogue which involves listening, counsel, comfort and forgiveness. The love of God is such that it can focus upon each individual without overlooking the rest. All who receive sacramental absolution ought to be able to feel *the warmth of this personal attention*. They should experience the intensity of the fatherly embrace offered to the prodigal son: "His father . . . embraced him and kissed him" (*Lk* 15:20).
>
> POPE SAINT JOHN PAUL II

are in doubt, it cannot hurt simply to confess what happened.

What is the difference between mortal sin and venial sin?

→ 316
How can we distinguish serious sins (mortal sins) from less serious (venial) sins?

The *Catechism* tells us venial sin is sin that "weakens charity", but does not break it, while mortal sin "destroys charity" in the soul (*CCC* 1855, 1863). This might not be easy to understand at first, but it might help if we look at a few examples. Catholic moral theologians say that a sin is venial if it lacks one of the three criteria mentioned before: seriousness, knowledge, and intention. So, for instance, if you get impatient with a friend and say something a little harsh, but without meaning any serious harm, that is a venial sin. But if you purposely say something *deeply* insulting to wound your friend—or, worse, if you do this behind his back with gossip—that might be a mortal sin. If it is, it should be confessed as soon as possible. Take another example, using the criterion of knowledge and ignorance. If someone raised as an atheist denies Jesus, he does this because he does not know better, so for him, it cannot be a mortal sin, even though it is clearly bad for his soul. However, if a believing Christian does the exact same thing, denying God just to fit in or to be funny, this could be very grave, especially if he somehow intends to hurt God. You can see the difference. Of course, venial sins need to be avoided, because they gradually harden our hearts and over time can lead to more serious sins if not attended to. Think again of the example of physical exercise: if skipping workouts becomes a more regular practice and you start eating unhealthy food, you eventually will once again be out of shape; likewise, indulging in venial sins weakens our spiritual "muscle", so to speak, and eventually can lead to more serious sin. Committing a venial sin versus a mortal sin is a bit like the difference between a slap to the face and a knife wound. One you can treat at home, the other requires immediate attention from the doctor. Venial sins can be confessed privately to God and God's forgiveness sought through prayer or penance, but mortal sins need the attention of a priest in the sacrament. A good priest will always be ready to help guide you concerning venial sins, too.

→ **1 Jn 5:16**

Many people say: "I don't need the Church's commandments. All I need is my conscience to tell me what's right and what's wrong." What would you say to them?

Personal conscience is incredibly important for the Church. Pope Pius XII called conscience "the most intimate, most secret

core of man". Yet conscience never works in a vacuum. Many factors in our lives work together to shape our sense of right and wrong, honing it, clearing it, warping it, or blocking it. The conscience is a bit like glass: it can be a long-distance camera lens, a beautiful bay window, a creepy fish-eye lens, or a dirty car windshield. The *Catechism* explains that we must spend our whole lives forming our conscience (*CCC* 1784), and the Church—given to the world by Jesus—is our surest teacher. Her only goal in giving us commandments and precepts is to guide us to joy and to love—"love that issues from a pure heart and a good conscience and sincere faith" (1 Tim 1:5).

How does the conscience work?

Our culture puts a big emphasis on feelings, and sometimes people equate their feelings with their conscience.

Feelings do matter, of course, but they are never the whole story. In reality, "conscience is a judgment of reason" (*CCC* 1778), prompting us to do what we *know* to be good. Feelings can be notoriously unreliable guides, especially when we are young. Think of Adam and Eve. Reason would have told them to respect God's one clear rule: do not eat from this one single tree in the garden. After all, they knew that God had created them and everything around them. But once the serpent came, their feelings of curiosity and doubt overwhelmed their right thinking. Interestingly, after they ate the fruit, they felt terrible, consumed by fear. This is a good illustration of how conscience works. Saint Thomas Aquinas teaches that virtue—the habit of doing good things—makes us happy, and indeed it does, but we have to use our realistic knowledge of what is right in order to get there. If an apparently good feeling runs against the truth, it is not really good. It takes time and practice to learn the difference, a process that Saint Ignatius of Loyola called the "discernment of spirits".

" When the enemy of our human nature tempts a just soul with his wiles and deceits, he wishes and desires that they be received and kept in secret. When they are revealed to a confessor . . . the enemy is greatly displeased for he knows that he cannot succeed in his evil design once his obvious deceits have been discovered.

SAINT IGNATIUS OF LOYOLA

→ 295 What is conscience?

How can I make sure that my conscience is as well formed as possible?

First of all, we simply have to learn what Christ teaches. This normally begins in the family or in religion class when we are children, but it is never, ever too late to start. Even bishops like me must keep exploring and going deeper. Jesus teaches us not only through the Bible, but through the Church, who helps us to understand Scripture more profoundly through Tradition and doctrine. There are many resources for learning about the Church Magisterium—books, podcasts, videos—but one of the best tools for young people today is the *YOUCAT*. Secondly, we have to look at the examples of good people, whether they are canonized saints, well-known Christians, or just acquaintances we respect. Sometimes Church doctrine can seem distant, so seeing this doctrine courageously lived out often makes it "real" for us. Thirdly, and just as importantly, we have to spend quiet time listening to God. It is not enough to know the "rules"; we must try to understand the reason behind them. When we truly believe that teachings are good, it becomes natural to follow them. If you have ever taken the time to learn to play basketball or piano, you know that it takes intense work, but the work becomes fun when

→ **297**
Can a person form his conscience?

you know there is a purpose, and the more you practice, the more second nature it becomes. The spiritual life is similar. Life is not about laws, but about a relationship with God, through Jesus. Only this relationship can give the rules any meaning.

What about sex? Many young people today are very confused and think that sex before marriage is normal. They want to try it out to see whether or not they make a good match. What would you say to them?

First, the fact that something is widespread doesn't make it "normal". Normal is God's intention for us—whether "everyone does it" or not. For example, virtually everyone has told a lie sometime, but that doesn't mean lying is normal, because we all deep down expect people to tell the truth. It is not only the right thing to do, but society depends on it. Now, you might ask, when it comes to sex, what is God's "normal"? Well, it is marriage. Sex is often called the "marital embrace", because it is meant to bring married couples close together, fusing them into one. It is sacred, and it involves the whole soul, as any faithful married couple can tell you. It also involves the real possibility of having children together. For these reasons, if you have sex with someone you aren't married to—even if you are seriously dating or engaged—you are fundamentally lying to them, because you have not yet offered them the real lifelong commitment that sex implies. Thus, the only true "safe sex" that exists is sex between husband and wife. And although it sounds harsh to modern ears, this is why the New Testament calls sex outside of marriage a grave sin (cf. 1 Cor 5:1). The world has trivialized the sexual union, but in God's plan, it is the crowning act of self-giving between spouses after their relationship has grown and deepened in other ways.

If I am in an improper sexual relationship and can't easily change it, can I even go to confession?

→ 408
How can you live as a young Christian if you are living in a premarital relationship or have already had premarital relations?

Once you're ready at least to try following God's commandments, go to confession and ask for help. Try. We should never give up on God's grace or on ourselves. Again, that would be despair, which is a temptation. If we earnestly want to live according to God's will, we can do the right thing even in situations that at first might seem unchangeable.

It is sometimes said that if you want to receive Communion, you should first go to confession. Should I go to confession before every Mass?

→ 230
What is penance?

Minimally, we only need to go to confession before Communion if we have committed a mortal sin. In fact, the *Catechism* says that the prayerful reception of the Eucharist itself "wipes away venial sins" (*CCC* 1394). Regular confession is important, but at a certain point, we have to put our trust in God's mercy and live in it. If we are struggling with some venial sin that irritates our conscience, there are many forms of penance in Christian life (see *CCC* 1434–1439). But sometimes people have tough cases. If you are in a dark period, going from mortal sin to mortal sin, then by all means, the confessional door is open for you. But so it is for all sinners, that is, all of us: it opens the door to the torrent of God's grace that purifies us and makes us happy. And so take heart: with regular confession, soon you will find freedom.

THE BASICS:

THE TEN COMMANDMENTS

1. I am the Lord, your God. You shall not have strange gods before me.
2. You shall not take the name of the Lord your God in vain.
3. You shall keep holy the Lord's day.
4. Honor your father and mother.
5. You shall not kill.
6. You shall not commit adultery.
7. You shall not steal.
8. You shall not bear false witness against your neighbor.
9. You shall not covet your neighbor's wife.
10. You shall not covet your neighbor's goods.

→ 349

THE DOUBLE COMMANDMENT OF LOVE

which our consciences can *always* follow

You shall love the Lord your God with all your heart, and with all your soul, and with all your mind.

You shall love your neighbor as yourself.

→ Mt 22:37, 39

Photo credits

Martin Buhl pp. 70, 79; Sylvia Buhl pp. 12, 34, 57, 63, 67, 80, 84; Peter Christoph Düren pp. 14–15; Vince Fleming (Unsplash) p. 89; Kilian Hasselmann p. 61; Kathleen Kasperson p. 77; Dennis Callahan p. 72; Luc Serafin pp. 8, 20, 26; Andreas Süss (*www.nightfever.org*) p. 6; © youmagazin pp. 42–43